crafted prayer

Other books by Graham Cooke

The Language of Love
The Secret of a Powerful Inner Life
Developing Your Prophetic Gifting
A Divine Confrontation

crafted prayer

*The Joy of Always
Getting Your Prayers Answered*

being with God series

Graham Cooke

Chosen
Grand Rapids, Michigan

Published by Chosen Books
A division of Baker Publishing Group
P.O. Box 6287, Grand Rapids, MI 49516–6287
www.chosenbooks.com

Originally published under the title *Crafted Prayer* by Sovereign
World Limited of Tonbridge, Kent, England

Printed in the United States of America

        Library of Congress Cataloging-in-Publication Data
Cooke, Graham.
    Crafted prayer : the joy of always getting your prayers
answered / Graham Cooke.
        p. cm. – (Being with God)
    Originally published: Tonbridge, Kent, England : Sovereign
World Ltd.
    ISBN 0-8007-9380-3 (pbk.)
    I. Prayer. I. Title.

BV210.3.C67 2004
248.3'2–dc22

                                                            2004050017

There is only one Person I can dedicate this book to—the Holy Spirit. I am constantly amazed at His wisdom, revelation and power in my life. I love His dedication to and passion for the Lord Jesus Christ. The way He reveals the Son to me has changed my life. His physical, emotional, mental and spiritual representation of the Father to me has continuously made me more excited and in awe of the great love of God for me.

contents

acknowledgments

Heather, Ben, Seth and Sophie: What a great, wacky family we are—I love it!

Carole Shiers, my personal assistant and faithful ministry partner for many, many years: thank you.

To the churches in Southampton (UK) and Vacaville (USA), which I call home, thank you, especially to my leaders, Billy and Caroline Kennedy (UK) and David and Deborah Crone (USA) for including us and being our friends.

To Tim and Darlene Dickerson, who graciously provide a home, support and, above all, true, loving friendship that withholds nothing. What a great blessing our relationship is for me and my family.

introduction

The time has come for a new way of prayer.
Paradoxically, this new method is actually an
ancient way of prayer, one in which God's faithful
servants like David and Paul flourished. I call it
"crafted prayer," and this book will teach you how
to make it a part of your life, too. The miracles I
have seen as a result of crafted prayer are too
numerous to record. There is such a joy in being
able to pray exactly what God wills for a person and
seeing His answer unfold before your very eyes. This
type of prayer can transform Christians, turning
what was a mundane prayer life bearing little fruit
into joyous, bridelike intercession. Allow me to
explain.

I believe God is taking many people into a new
season of intimate, bridelike prayer. Real warfare in
the Kingdom of God is always concerned with the
battle for intimacy. This is a time to come off the
battlefield and enter a new place of intimate

petition. Too many intercessors have become exhausted and too burned out to continue praying the way the Church has been advocating. As we learn to become conformed to God and His nature and are transformed in our minds and personalities, He will teach us to look beyond the natural into the supernatural realm and see the Kingdom of heaven at work in every need. It will no longer matter what life, people or even the enemy throw at us, because we will be able to hear the conversation in heaven and understand that God is at work all around us.

I believe God is raising up an army of Esthers, an army of bridal intercessors, and it is a time to come off the wall and rest in the throne-room presence of God—in our secret place in Him. It will be difficult for some people to come out of ministry and move into the discipline of resting in God, but the discipline of rest must be entered; it is a time of laying down ministry to gain fresh intimacy.

Do not pray with importunity but with delight and favor. Do not pray against the enemy, but let your delighted prayers cause the King to stir Himself and come down. God's anointing will cause you to intercede with joy so that His glory will fill the earth. What is the glory of God? In Exodus 33:18–19, when Moses asked God to show His glory,

God said He would cause His goodness to pass before him. One of the glories of God, therefore, is that He is good!

As bridal intercessors, it will be our joy and delight to pray for the goodness of God to come down so that the Church can learn that we really do overcome evil with good. The Holy Spirit will give us a new strategy for prayer and perseverance, one that contains delight and laughter and is full of ardent and passionate love, bathed in fresh worship and birthed out of a deeper intimacy. I believe crafted prayer is part of this shift.

As we come and petition the Lord out of this place of closeness, He will be pleased to speak into our hearts His favor and blessing. Not only will our prayers move His heart and hands, but the words we receive from Him will be like a balm of Gilead across the nations, and churches will rise up in fresh favor. The attention of the Church will be taken off the enemy and be put on the King of Kings.

Let us pray that a revelation of the Lord's love for us would fill our hearts, that we may come into a whole new place of spirituality, a whole new place of walking with Him, where we will be convinced that God loves us, cares for us and is for us—and that He wants us to succeed. Amen!

crafted prayer

Jesus preached, "And whatever things you ask in prayer, believing, you will receive" (Matthew 21:22). Why, then, do we seemingly receive so few answers to prayer today? Was Jesus lying to us? Of course not! The issue, then, must be our own—we must not believe what we are praying.

Prayer, as it is taught in most churches, does not work. Most of us have been brought up in a tradition that when something bad happens, prayer must begin immediately. This seems reasonable and even righteous, but on a deeper level, it actually hinders the power of God to work on our behalf. In my experience in churches and friendships, I have seen that when we pray too soon, we usually pray in unbelief. We find ourselves praying out of the shock or trauma of the situation itself, and we pray out of our panic, worry, anxiety and concern.

For example, a church member is diagnosed with a serious illness. Immediately, our compassion rises up, and we burst into prayer. We use a shotgun approach, spraying heaven with every imaginable request. *Well, Father, I pray this,* we start. Then another thought enters our mind, so we switch tracks: *Oh, Father, I pray that.* Doubt attacks us and our prayer shifts again: *Well, Lord, if it be Your will, I pray this,* and *Father, I pray that you might want to think about doing this.* Our love for the person involved prompts us to remind God of how valuable the person is to God: *Well, Lord, you know he is a faithful servant.* God now has to sift through a blizzard of prayer thrown up within a few minutes, a storm further thickened if there is more than one intercessor. You can forgive God for sitting there and thinking, *What is this? Multiple choice?*

> "Don't pray to escape trouble. Don't pray to be comfortable in your emotions. Pray to do the will of God in every situation. Nothing else is worth praying for."
> —Samuel M. Shoemaker

Sadly, our prayers have stopped being about the person in need and have become our effort to try to find God. We have forgotten to pray what God actually wants to do and have begun our own search for Him. We should not be using prayer to find God—that is what thanksgiving is for. The Bible is clear—it is not with prayer that we enter His gates, but with thanksgiving.

The apostle Paul wrote, "Rejoice always, pray without ceasing, in everything give thanks; for this is the will of God in Christ Jesus for you" (1 Thessalonians 5:16–18). Prayer, in the initial stage, is not about speaking. It is about listening and reading. It is about thanking God because, of the billions of people who walk the earth, Christians are supposed to be the most relaxed and the most grateful. We are called to be the Disneyland of faiths—the happiest people on earth. Even on the toughest days, the joy of the Lord is a force of strength for us. If we are filled with the fullness of God, we behave in ways unlike the world around us. There is no place for worry or panic in a Christian's life. Faith and anxiety cannot exist in the same space at the same time. One of them has to go, and you have the power to choose which.

We must come before God with thanksgiving, but He is not asking us to become a supernatural masochist: "Oh, I thank You, Lord, that I have crashed my car." No! What we are thanking God for is the reality of His presence. "I will never leave you nor forsake you," God promised in Hebrews 13:5.

thanksgiving

We can thank God first, in every situation, because every problem we encounter comes with His provision attached to it. God has a plan and a purpose for us; He says that everything works together for those who love Him. That promise is a deep well of provision for us. Whatever calamity life throws at us, God can use it for our blessing and our benefit. Paul wrote, "And we know that all things work together for good to those who love God, to those who are the called according to His purpose" (Romans 8:28). It is that attribute of God's nature that makes it so critical for us to come to a place of thanksgiving. By our entering His presence in the midst of a problem, He can act on our behalf. Our heart may be all over the place, but there is a central place of truth where we gather—in the goodness of God.

"Sometimes we make praise a prisoner to our emotions rather than a way of releasing our inner self to God."
—Graham Cooke

David sang, "Let us come before His presence with thanksgiving; let us shout joyfully to Him with psalms" (Psalm 95:2). At all times, we need to rejoice, praying something like this: *Thank You that You are with me in this. I don't know how You're*

going to work it out, but I know You're with me
because You said You would be, and that's enough
for me. I don't have to feel Your presence—Your word
is enough. Thank You.

Gratitude is the bedrock of our life and worship.
Often we fail to worship during the week, thinking
Sundays or conferences are our times to worship.
But worship is a part of everyday life. When we
come before God, we must be thankful. We need to
practice being grateful a lot more than we do. What
are Christians supposed to sound like
on the earth? Our voices should be
heard, at all times, worshiping God.
If our worship is built on a
foundation of thankfulness, we must
have a vision and a passion to be
grateful. We also need a plan, for vision without
strategy is just wishful thinking. We need to plan to
enter God's presence with our thanksgiving, not our
prayer: *Thank You, Lord. I don't know how You're*
going to work this thing out, but I know You will.
I praise You. I worship You. And once we've come
into His presence, we need to be still and listen to
the heart of God.

"It is in the process
of being worshipped that
God communicates His
presence to men."
—C. S. Lewis

stillness

Being still opens a channel of communication between us and heaven. All of us have a background conversation going on in our minds. Head noise, as my friend and British psychologist Jim McNeish calls it, is an internal voice, a soundtrack for our lives. It is similar to a special feature on a DVD—an ongoing, one-way, stream-of-consciousness conversation, commenting on our life as it unfolds. Stillness is not about getting somewhere quiet, although that often helps, but about stilling those voices in our heads. It takes discipline to quiet those voices, but we must do it. And we can do it, because God is with us.

It is this initial head noise that we convert into "prayers" when we rush too quickly into intercession. Because we have not stilled ourselves, we pray in our own strength, and we come to God's door under the weight and panic of the circumstances facing us. We speak often and are rarely still—in fact, we are the opposite of God.

God is always still and rarely speaks, so there is a difference between the Lord speaking *in* us and the Lord speaking *to* us. When we say, "Oh, God spoke to me," what has normally happened is that out of the storehouse of words, thoughts, meditations, conversations and Scripture we carry in our spirit, God has selected something previously said to us and brought it back into our consciousness. Like a computer user loading a file, God pulls up the treasure He has already saved in us. *Oh yeah,* we think. *That makes sense. That's the Lord speaking.* God punctuates His silence with words, and when God speaks, it is an event. When He speaks to us, something is imparted. His presence is profound. He spoke once, and the whole earth was created. When God speaks, something happens, something is shaken, something is created and produced. When the Lord speaks to us, there is always a dynamic residue of His presence that remains with us—it is a signature moment!

God told David, "Be still, and know that I am God" (Psalm 46:10). It was a word that brought a profound sense of the presence of God to David in what were difficult circumstances. It is interesting that Psalm 46 begins with an earthquake and ends with "Be still." Only God can talk about stillness in the midst of an earthquake. When the whole landscape of your life is shifting beneath your feet, only God can say, "Be still, and know that I am God."

Knowledge of God comes through peace and stillness. God wants to send us into battle, but if we do not find stillness beforehand, how will we ever find peace in the fight? Rest is our best weapon against the enemy, because rest allows us to hide in our secret place in God. The devil hates us with a malevolence and malignancy that is unimaginable, but he is not stupid—he won't chase us into the Holy of Holies, the very presence of God, because he knows who he is going to meet there. We need to learn how to use God as our refuge, as our fortress, as our high place, as our secret place where the enemy cannot touch us. If the enemy cannot find us, he cannot hurt us. God has provided us a secret place in Him.

"Peace is the potting soil of revelation."
—John Paul Jackson

I once had a dream about secret places. It was one of those dreams that seemed to last for days. A band of thirty vile and evil warriors were chasing me through what looked like the African bush. If you've seen *The Lord of the Rings,* they looked a bit like those evil Orcs. I was running, sword in hand, up hills, down into valleys, through rivers, across meadows, even through a desert, and these Orcs were constantly chasing me, yapping like dogs. I was exhausted, at the limit of my strength. I began to scan the land ahead for a place to fight and make a last, desperate stand.

In the distance, I saw something shimmering, so I ran toward it. It looked like a shower rail, suspended by itself and covered with a thin, almost transparent, material. I had the oddest impulse to stand inside it. I do not why I did it, but when I got into it, I could see right through it and could see the enemy getting closer and closer. I reached for my sword but heard a voice: "Be still." I put my sword back. The Orcs got closer, and my hand again twitched toward the sword. "Be still," the voice said, chuckling. "Be still." My panic subsided until I heard them just a quarter of a mile away. I moved for my sword again. "Grae," the voice chuckled, "be still."

So I put my hands by my sides and waited, heart hammering in my chest. The enemy broke through into the clearing and came at me, and I braced myself for death. Suddenly, I felt arms wrap around me and God's voice whisper in my ear, "It's okay. Be still." They came right at me, and then, unbelievably, inexplicably, they parted and flowed around me, like a river around an island. It was like they had never seen me. I turned around and watched as they ran into the distance.

"What was all that about?" I asked.

And all I heard in my heart was, "Grae, when you're in your secret place, there's nothing from the enemy that can actually touch you. He doesn't even know how to locate you. He can run right at you and not even see you." Our secret place is like a *Star Trek* cloaking device—it renders us invisible to the enemy's sensors and attacks. I woke up from that dream and meditated on it for days. *I am never going to be anxious again,* I thought. *I am just going to step into that secret place and learn to live there, even if it kills me.*

You have to lose your ability to panic if you are going to walk with God. You have to lose your ability to worry if you are going to walk with God. There is a secret place set aside for each of us. God is love, and in His love, He has set aside a place where we can live in Him no matter what. He loves to teach people where that place is, because when His children get into their secret place, they can enjoy life fully. It does not matter what comes against them—they rise to the challenge. Without stillness, our experience of God is limited. Stillness is the precursor to rest in the Lord, a spiritual discipline drawing us into a continual experience of His presence. It is this rest, this stillness, this secret place of God, that releases unbroken communion with Him—it releases what the Bible calls "unceasing prayer."

how to get answers

Before we pray, we need to meditate. Prayer, in its simplest form, is finding out what God wants to do and then asking Him to do it. One of the best ways to get a fix on God's heart for us is to read His Scripture. The apostle John writes, "Now this is the confidence that we have in Him, that if we ask anything according to His will, He hears us. And if we know that He hears us, whatever we ask, we know that we have the petitions that we have asked of Him" (1 John 5:14–15). To see your prayers answered, enter God's presence with thanksgiving and worship. Then rest in your secret place and meditate on His Scripture and words to you. Ask the Lord, *What do You want to do in these circumstances?* Then listen and wait until the Lord answers and directs you how to pray.

We find this principle in the book of Romans:

> Likewise the Spirit also helps in our weaknesses. For we do not know what we should pray for as we ought, but the Spirit Himself makes intercession for us with groanings which cannot be uttered. Now He who searches the hearts knows what the mind of the Spirit is, because He makes intercession for the

saints according to the will of God. And we know that all things work together for good to those who love God, to those who are the called according to His purpose. For whom He foreknew, He also predestined to be conformed to the image of His Son, that He might be the firstborn among many brethren. Moreover whom He predestined, these He also called; whom He called, these He also justified; and whom He justified, these He also glorified.

What then shall we say to these things? If God is for us, who can be against us? He who did not spare His own Son, but delivered Him up for us all, how shall He not with Him also freely give us all things? Who shall bring a charge against God's elect? It is God who justifies. Who is he who condemns? It is Christ who died, and furthermore is also risen, who is even at the right hand of God, who also makes intercession for us. Who shall separate us from the love of Christ? Shall tribulation, or distress, or persecution, or famine, or nakedness, or peril, or sword? As it is written:

"For Your sake we are killed all day long;
We are accounted as sheep for the slaughter."

Yet in all these things we are more than conquerors through Him who loved us. For I am persuaded that neither death nor life, nor angels nor principalities nor powers, nor things present nor things to come, nor height nor depth, nor any other created thing, shall be able to separate us from the love of God which is in Christ Jesus our Lord.

Romans 8:26–39

The Holy Spirit helps us to pray in our weakness, yet, traditionally, we haven't been very concerned with what He is praying. Suppose I said to you, "The Lord has given me an excellent prophetic word for you," and then I turned around and left the room. In all likelihood, you would chase me: "What? What's the word?" Of course you would want to know the word—it is human nature.

If I said to you that, right now, the Holy Spirit is interceding for you according to God's will, what would your question be? "What's He praying?" of course. And if I added, "By the way, Jesus is at the right hand of the Father right now, and He's praying for you, too," you would ask, "What's He praying?" and "Do He and the Holy Spirit agree?"

> "Prayer is finding out what God wants to do and asking Him to do it!"

Paul's words in Romans 8:26 are powerful: "For we do not know what we should pray for as we ought, but the Spirit Himself makes intercession for us." The Father says to the Holy Spirit, "This is what

I want for Graham. Ask Me to do it." So He prays for me in the will of God, while I knock about the earth, not sure of how to pray for myself. Who is my friend at this point in time? Who is my tutor? Who is my comforter? What is His name? The Holy Spirit! Only He can help me with my weakness in prayer.

Now that you know you have a Person dedicated to improving your prayer life, don't you want to work with Him? The Spirit helps us to pray by revealing the will of God. When we pray in line with what the Holy Spirit is doing, what are we doing? We are not praying, trying to find an answer, but praying *with* the answer. For too long we have been satisfied to use prayer to try to find God. That is not what prayer is for—prayer is asking God to do the very thing He is telling us He wants to do. It comes with a confidence in our heart that because we've heard the will of God, we know we are praying what He wants, and He will answer.

I have seen this power work, firsthand, time after time. One example hits especially close to home for me, as it involved a friend of mine. David (not his real name) was a missionary in Africa when the Lord showed me, in prayer, what David would go through in the next season of his life. The regime David was living under (which I cannot divulge for security reasons) was actually opposed to missionaries—it saw them as servants of Western imperialism.

The Lord indicated that David would be attacked physically and be beaten. His car would be stolen, his church and medical clinic would be ransacked and his family and congregation would be threatened. In all of this, however, if David stood his ground in peace and refused to see the people as enemies, then the Lord would give him favor with God and man through a particular opportunity to minister powerfully in the supernatural (something David was not noted for in his ministry!). That supernatural event would open unimaginable doors.

I had no freedom to prophesy these things to David; only permission to intercede for him. There are times in the prophetic ministry when words we receive for others must stay in the throne room. In this instance, they are more powerful when converted into crafted prayer and spoken to the Father than when put into prophetic language and ministered to human beings.

> "Submission to God's will is the softest pillow on which to rest."
> —Unknown

I crafted a prayer for David and interceded before the Lord until the burden lifted. We must learn to pray until God says, "Enough!" Sometimes they are "PUSH" prayers, where we Pray

Until Something Happens. At other times, we pray until God tells us to stop or until we have an assurance He has heard and will act.

The result of this particular scenario was that David found favor with the Lord. One of his leading opponents, a formidable adversary, had a firstborn son who was diagnosed with a serious disease. No medical help was available. Without this vital treatment, the son would die painfully. During a period of awful oppressive activity against the mission, David was summoned to face his great rival. During an intense interrogation, David felt compelled (his own words) to offer to pray for the son of his antagonist.

Needless to say, the boy was healed, the mission was saved and David's former opponent is now providing him with resources!

The change in David has been remarkable. Through these circumstances, God has fashioned a man of courage, conviction, humility and power. He has moved into a level of supernatural gifting that has resulted in an evangelistic breakthrough for the work. Although still living at the whim of this despotic character (who has not changed!), David is

"God allows in His wisdom what He could easily prevent by His power."
—Graham Cooke

tolerated and even encouraged in his ministry to that people group.

All of the things I felt prompted to pray for in this circumstance have happened, and out of oppression and adversity, God has produced a work no one can deny or stop!

When I shared my initial perceptions and my crafted prayers with David, they were more powerful to him than an actual prophetic word. If I had told him sooner, he would have become fearful and distressed and would simply not have endured the struggle. His fear, especially for his family, would have dominated his faith.

There are precedents in Scripture for this type of situation. Consider Acts 20:22–23: "And see, now I go bound in the spirit to Jerusalem, not knowing the things that will happen to me there, except that the Holy Spirit testifies in every city, saying that chains and tribulations await me."

On one hand, the Lord revealed and confirmed to Paul the dangers awaiting him. On the other, he had no clue what the result would be. Interestingly enough, no one felt compelled to exercise authority over the situation. Paul, however, knew the will of God for his time in

"Key ministries do not rescue God's people from legitimate struggle."
—Graham Cooke

Jerusalem and presumably could craft prayers that would align himself with God's greater purpose. He definitely knew that the peace of God, which passes all understanding, would prevent anxiety and guard his heart (see Philippians 4:7).

heavenly dialogue

The other scriptural insight compatible with this type of situation is found in Luke 22:31–32: "And the Lord said, 'Simon, Simon! Indeed, Satan has asked for you, that he may sift you as wheat. But I have prayed for you, that your faith should not fail; and when you have returned to Me, strengthen your brethren.'"

Jesus could simply have taken authority over the enemy and have prevented the situation from happening. But He recognized that it was important for Simon Peter to struggle through to a deeper place of faith and relationship. Simon had to discover something profound about himself and also the love of God for him.

God wants us to know what He is praying. Jesus went to Simon Peter and explained that Satan wanted to sift Jesus' disciple like wheat. "But I have prayed for you," Jesus said. In what might have been the most significant moment of Peter's life, Jesus told him what He was praying for: "That your faith should not fail; and when you have returned to Me, strengthen your brethren." Peter, who later became a pillar of the Church, knew that this attack of the enemy was not going to stop him. In fact, it was going to make him strong enough to be a help to his brothers. Satan wanted to beat him, but in heaven there was a different plan and conversation unfolding.

The Western Church, in my belief, has a flawed understanding of the Trinity. We picture a large figure of authority (the Father), a medium figure of grace (Jesus) and a bird (the Holy Spirit)! Inadvertently, we downgrade the Holy Spirit's power in our life—what can a bird do, after all?

I greatly prefer the Eastern Church's view of the Trinity: three equals, sitting at a round table and talking. If Jesus is sitting at the right hand of the Father, interceding, and the Holy Spirit is there, praying according to the will of God, then there must be a conversation going on among the Three. Don't you wonder what they are saying about you in any given situation? What is the conversation in heaven over

> "There will be no peace as long as God remains unseated at the conference table."
> —Unknown

your life right now? By exploring and seeking out this heavenly dialogue, we can learn what God's will is for a situation and, by extension, what we should be praying.

By seeking the conversation in heaven for ourselves, we embark on a great spiritual adventure where we are conformed to the will of God. It is a fascinating way to live, because it allows us to rise above our circumstances and pray in line with a God who adores us and wants us to be supremely confident in doing His will. He wants us to find joy in our situation and to understand that nothing out there can beat us, because of who He is in us. By listening in to the conversation in heaven, we learn that a single situation can have massive repercussions on a number of people. Isaiah listened to the conversation in heaven and discovered the will of God for himself (see Isaiah 6). We become a prophetic voice in that circle, proclaiming and declaring God's will, and praying it out. *What else are You up to?* we ask God. *I know You—You don't just do one thing!* God is always doing fifteen or twenty things around our lives, and by seeking out His will before we pray, He shows us His works-in-progress.

Amazingly, we will find that God is working in the most unlikely people and the most difficult situations. As we prove ourselves faithful in the little prayers and issues, God gives us greater favor to pray out His will. We look at Uncle Will and Aunt Jean and God gives us a prayer for them—not just for the single issue they are facing, but a complete, whole prayer. Suddenly, our prayer lives are electric with excitement, and we cannot drag ourselves away from intercession!

"You need to rejoice, guys, and then pray without ceasing," Paul told the Thessalonians. Unceasing prayer comes when a person has found the will of God and prays until the situation reflects what He wants to do. Intercessors like that already know the outcome of the time they have invested in prayer, so they pray with joy and excitement. It does not matter how long it takes for the situation to resolve itself—our prayer is about all the other stuff God is doing while He is waiting for that moment to come. We just pray without ceasing.

How do we listen in on that conversation in heaven? First, we enter God's presence with thanksgiving. Then we still ourselves, finding and resting in that secret place He has set aside for us. God will reveal Himself to us in a number of ways. We have Scripture because it tells us what the heart and mind of God is in certain situations. It is like a heavenly cheat sheet. God has given us a book full of His words, and the Holy Spirit will lead us to a particular passage. *Hmmm,* we will think as we read it.

Yes, God will reply. *Use that as a base, because My heart's in that for you right now.*

The answer may come in another way, in a dream or an impression. I suggest looking back through your personal journal or considering prophetic words already given to you. Sometimes we ask God to say something He has already said—we can use ingredients from older prophetic words in our prayer.

God is very generous and the kindest Person I have ever met. He wants us to know what His will is. He longs to release His children from worry and fear. He desires to show us what He is doing in a situation and in our lives. He hungers for us to pray what He is praying.

crafting our prayer

Prayer is not meant to be used like a fisherman's net to trawl for the will of God. Instead, we use prayer to pray the will of God, and that brings us into a place of faith and proclamation. We grow in confidence in

Crafted Prayer

My child, the weapons of your warfare are more than a match
for the enemy.
Whatever has made you feel small can be turned around with
the right weapon.

Child, this is not an equal fight!
Every small thing I give you is a significant weapon against your
adversary.
The odds are always in your favor.

Remain childlike and simple in your walk with Me.
I want you to enjoy these experiences I send to you.
Through them I will teach you to smile, to laugh and to enjoy
the power of your Sovereign Lord.

This next season, everything will start to fall into place for you.
Only look at everything through the eyes and a heart of a
trusting child.
You are My special treasure, my precious one. I have set this
next phase of your journey aside for the purpose of you
walking in simplicity and adoration of Me ... enjoy!

the will of God as our prayers change us to be more like Him. We have decided to follow the process God has ordained in the circumstances He has allowed to unfold.

Paul wrote, "For whom He foreknew, He also predestined to be conformed to the image of His Son" (Romans 8:29). In every situation, there is a pathway that enables us to become more like Jesus.

A part of our prayer initiative is to find what it is that God wants us to do to become more like Him. There is always an area of our lives where we need to become more like Christ, and the Lord is saying to us, *If you will follow the way I want you to pray, you will not only have the answer to that prayer, but you will grow in Me. There is a predestined, predetermined thing I want you to become in every situation—I want to give you more of Myself.*

> "I know the plans I have for you ... to give you a future and a hope."
> —God, through Jeremiah

Every obstacle, every problem, every attack is allowed and designed to teach you to become more like Jesus. That is why every problem comes with a provision attached to it. As Christians, we must stand in the midst of the problem, knowing God's promise, and expect a provision. All things work together for good in the economy of God. There are no Great Depressions or stock market crashes. Paul asked, "Who shall separate us from the love of Christ?" (Romans 8:35). Nothing, he answered: "Neither death nor life, nor angels nor principalities nor powers, nor things present nor things to come, nor height nor depth, nor any other created thing, shall be able to separate us from the love of God which is in Christ Jesus our Lord" (verses 38–39). I am convinced, in fact, that all the things Paul mentioned are actually designed to reveal God's love for us.

When we craft a prayer, our crisis becomes an opportunity for God to work. Everything is useful to our growth in the Spirit because God is for us in every situation. Look at the list of what cannot separate us from the love of God: accusation, condemnation, tribulation, distress, persecution, famine, exposure, peril, the sword, death, life, angels, principalities, things present, things to come, height and depth. It does not matter how big and powerful the thing against us is—God has made us more than conquerors. Prayer is about certainty. There should be boldness in our hearts when we pray, for heaven is listening to our prayers. Everything in God's heart wants to tell us, *This is what I want to do. Pray like this.*

Jesus said, "Therefore I say to you, whatever things you ask when you pray, believe that you receive them, and you will have them" (Mark 11:24). When we pray in the will of God, whatever we ask will be given. There is no difference between an anointed prayer and an unanointed prayer. Prayer is prayer to God. Sometimes our emotions are present with our faith; other times, they are not. Fortunately, God is so good that He will look at us, even when we are so lost we cannot put a prayer into words, and say, *Just groan—I'll understand what you mean. I promise.* God can and does interpret our groans.

Crafted prayer is a wonderful tool. We can look at our situation, take time to study the Word, take time for thanksgiving and bring our heart into line with what God wants to do. Then we craft a prayer that covers the whole issue. Write your prayers out, over and over, until you feel them seep into your heart. Write them with your friends, helping one another, learning from one another and inspiring one another. Then commit yourself to praying the crafted prayer.

The whole point of crafted prayer is that it releases God's greatness in us, making us great. What is the glory of His inheritance? The glory of

Israel going into the Promised Land was that God's
presence went with them. No one could stand
against God's greatness in them. This is who we are.
We have to get our hearts and minds out of a
poverty mindset of spirituality and into a place
where we understand that the majesty of God and
the majesty of His Church is the same thing. We are
the people of God, and nothing can come against us.
We must be a confident people and know that God is
for us. It is our identity, our destiny, our inheritance.
No weapon fashioned against the Church will
prosper! God's power is here. "Every place that the
sole of your foot will tread upon I have given you,"
God said (Joshua 1:3). The Church is destined for
victory!

It is time to use prayer to turn the tables on the
enemy. We can make the devil tired, weary,
depressed, discouraged, exhausted and in need of
psychiatric care. In fact, we can wear him out
exactly as he has worn the Church out. Where is this
place of vengeance and favor Jesus spoke about
when He read His inheritance word, Isaiah 61? You
have favor with God and man, and your vengeance
is that God will turn around every attack the enemy
throws at you and use it to bless you.

Listen to this promise from the book of Ephesians:

For this reason I bow my knees to the Father of our
Lord Jesus Christ, from whom the whole family in
heaven and earth is named, that He would grant
you, according to the riches of His glory, to be
strengthened with might through His Spirit in the
inner man, that Christ may dwell in your hearts
through faith; that you, being rooted and grounded
in love, may be able to comprehend with all the
saints what is the width and length and depth and
height—to know the love of Christ which passes
knowledge; that you may be filled with all the
fullness of God.

Now to Him who is able to do exceedingly
abundantly above all that we ask or think,
according to the power that works in us, to Him be
glory in the church by Christ Jesus to all
generations, forever and ever.

Ephesians 3:14–21

God wants to strengthen you with power through
His Spirit. He dreams of you being confident, bold
and joyful, because you walk with Him who knows
and sees and does everything. Your understanding
of who God is for you will grow until it fills you,
and you have more confidence than you know
what to do with. In fact, you can be so full of God
that no one around will be able to stand in unbelief.

In our little bodies, there can be the confidence and anointing to take an entire community for God. One person with the Lord is always on the side with the power and the victory. Whom would you rather have on your side—a thousand people who cannot kill one, or one person who can kill a thousand?

We are too used to mediocrity, to thinking in small things, but are called to more than that. We have met Jesus, a Man who is incredibly powerful, deeply intentional and overwhelmingly confident. Nothing fazes Him, nothing worries Him. He is so full of joy that He even sings over His people. He looks at the enemy and laughs. "Is that all you've got?" He says. "Just bring it!" We have made allowances for losing, but a good fight is one we win. If we could just learn to walk with God in the way He wants, we would be victorious, again and again.

Ephesians 3:14–21 is a prayer about identifying with the Father and being strengthened by Him on the inside. God's will is that Christ would dwell within us, rooting us in His love. His children are supposed to be eagles, soaring on the wind, but we are all too content to be chickens. Fullness is our destiny, but emptiness is our crutch. We must shake this weakness off, once and for all. In Christ, we are God's champions, born to proclaim and declare His greatness and His goodness. We are meant to be an inspired people who live in confidence. We are not arrogant or overbearing, but cheerful and confident in God's provision for us. The joy of the Lord truly is our strength.

Crafted prayer brings us to a confident focus on God so that the enemy cannot trap us in fear and doubt. The enemy always uses the same line first: "Has God said?" With a crafted prayer, we can flip over a piece of paper and shoot back, "Well, God has said it, thank you very much. Here is His prayer right here!" I love crafted prayer and the comfort the Holy Spirit packages with it. I love the faith that remains in me when I pray the things God has told me I can pray. I love persevering in prayer—it has become a pleasure, not a chore.

David's journal

Prayer was a similar pleasure for David, as we can see in his journal, which is found in the book of Psalms. Many of his psalms are crafted prayers. Take Psalm 51, for example, a passage David wrote after the prophet Nathan came to David and exposed his adultery with Bathsheba and his hand in the murder of Uriah the Hittite.

Imagine for a moment the conversation going on in heaven over this situation. The Father, Son and Holy Spirit are seated at a round table, looking at David, who is feeling ashamed and condemned. David is humiliated and feels about an inch high. His heart is broken, and he is worried God is going to remove the Holy Spirit from him. He wants to be cleansed.

Imagine the conversation the Trinity is having: "Well, you know, he needs to understand My grace. He needs to learn about loving-kindness. He needs to know that I have compassion for him. He needs to be washed, cleansed and purified. He needs to learn that there is truth in the inner man. He needs wisdom from here on high. He needs to be restored, and he definitely needs the joy of his salvation restored."

It goes on: "He needs to know that I'm going to block out his transgressions. I can give him a clean heart, a steadfast spirit, and I'm not going to take the Holy Spirit away from him."

That, let us assume, was the conversation in heaven. David, broken, sat down and began to write his prayer, listening to what God wanted him to pray:

Have mercy upon me, O God,
According to Your lovingkindness;
According to the multitude of Your tender mercies,
Blot out my transgressions.
Wash me thoroughly from my iniquity,
And cleanse me from my sin.

For I acknowledge my transgressions,
And my sin is always before me.
Against You, You only, have I sinned,
And done this evil in Your sight—
That You may be found just when You speak,
And blameless when You judge.

Behold, I was brought forth in iniquity,
And in sin my mother conceived me.
Behold, You desire truth in the inward parts,
And in the hidden part You will make me to know
       wisdom.

Purge me with hyssop, and I shall be clean;
Wash me, and I shall be whiter than snow.
Make me hear joy and gladness,
That the bones You have broken may rejoice.
Hide Your face from my sins,
And blot out all my iniquities.

Create in me a clean heart, O God,
And renew a steadfast spirit within me.

Do not cast me away from Your presence,
And do not take Your Holy Spirit from me.
Restore to me the joy of Your salvation,
And uphold me by Your generous Spirit.

Psalm 51:1–12

Do you see how all the key words from the
conversation in heaven have found themselves in
David's psalm? There is symmetry between what
God wants to do and what David prayed. As Jesus
prayed, "Let it be done on earth, as it is in heaven."
Eventually, David received an answer to his prayer
and was set free from his sin.

We see another of David's crafted prayers in
Psalm 57. At the time, David was not yet king. He
had been anointed king by Samuel many years
before, but Saul was still chasing him around the
wilderness, trying to kill him. David was hiding in
caves, rarely sleeping in the same place twice. He
was leading a ragtag band of mercenaries, some of
whom would possibly have loved to turn him in and
collect the reward Saul was offering. Throughout the
countryside, others were watching for him, also
looking to ingratiate themselves with King Saul.
Whom could David trust? Why was it so hard to
become king, when Samuel himself had prophesied

it would happen? What was the conversation in heaven over this issue?

Again, the Trinity was sitting at their table, talking: "David needs to know I'm his refuge. He's hanging out in caves, and using that as a refuge, but he needs to know truly that I want to be his protection and his refuge. There is mercy for him. He needs to know that if he calls out to Me, I will save him. I'm with him, and I'm against his enemies. I want to give him a steadfast heart. He needs to learn how to use his circumstances to awaken praise and worship in his life, because that will bring him confidence. Let's teach him how to use these circumstances to bring himself to a place of exaltation."

Now read this crafted prayer of David, and see if you can spot the moment the prayer turns into a crafted psalm of thanksgiving—that is what crafted prayers do when they are prayed in confidence. We cannot pray in the will of God with confidence and not have our hearts turned toward praise.

> Be merciful to me, O God, be merciful to me!
> For my soul trusts in You;
> And in the shadow of Your wings I will make my
>   refuge,
> Until these calamities have passed by.

I will cry out to God Most High,
To God who performs all things for me.
He shall send from heaven and save me;
He reproaches the one who would swallow me up.
    Selah
God shall send forth His mercy and His truth.

My soul is among lions;
I lie among the sons of men
Who are set on fire,
Whose teeth are spears and arrows,
And their tongue a sharp sword.
Be exalted, O God, above the heavens;
Let Your glory be above all the earth.

They have prepared a net for my steps;
My soul is bowed down;
They have dug a pit before me;
Into the midst of it they themselves have fallen.
    Selah

My heart is steadfast, O God, my heart is steadfast;
I will sing and give praise.
Awake, my glory!
Awake, lute and harp!
I will awaken the dawn.

I will praise You, O Lord, among the peoples;
I will sing to You among the nations.

For Your mercy reaches unto the heavens,
And Your truth unto the clouds.
Be exalted, O God, above the heavens;
Let Your glory be above all the earth.

Psalm 57

The psalm takes its turn into thanksgiving at the line, "My heart is steadfast, O God, my heart is steadfast." It is the destiny of all Christians to have their prayers, if prayed in the will of God, answered. It is part of our inheritance to be, above all, secure and confident in the will of God.

presumption

It is not, however, part of our inheritance to be presumptuous of what God's will is. The first question we have to ask in any crafted prayer is what God's plan is. "Is this life or is this death?" We must first understand His will, even if we do not initially agree with it. We must ask the tough questions; we cannot write a crafted prayer out of presumption.

I had another friend, George (not his real name), who was deathly ill. His church and family had been praying and praying, but he had deteriorated badly.

While I was away, traveling, the Lord showed me that George's time was ending. He was going to die.

When I returned home, I went to see George. He was in a bed, surrounded by his loved ones. He looked at me and asked the most difficult question of his life: "Don't lie to me, Grae. Am I going to live or die?"

"Have a great death," I gently and lovingly told him. George's family was horrified and sat stunned. George was also silent for a few moments.

"Grae, I'm going to have the greatest death you've ever seen," he replied.

Immediately, the atmosphere in the room changed. George made up a list of 24 people—friends, neighbors, co-workers and nurses—whom he wanted to see. His attitude brightened. Nurses and physicians began to ask to stay with him because they loved being there. God was not going to heal George, but the two had entered into a fellowship of suffering; there was much grace in the room.

One by one, George met with the people on his list. One by one, each accepted Christ. Death had become George's stepping-stone, literally and physically, into a different place with God. The 24th person on his list was a veteran nurse whom he asked to come and sit with him during his final hours. It took some convincing, but she came. That night, they talked about life, death and God. Severely weakened, George suddenly sat bolt upright. With a huge smile on his face, and a peaceful heart, he told her how excited he was to see Jesus. It was his final moment in this world. The nurse was stunned by the whole experience. She fell to her knees and accepted Jesus. George had led 24 people to Christ during his final days. His funeral was a lively celebration of the life of a man who had changed people's worlds. There was no black; in fact, George had asked everyone to wear Hawaiian shirts.

There will be times when it will be difficult to craft a prayer. Our natural inclination will be to pray for what we think is best. We must resist that presumption and discover what God's will is.

a testimony

Crafted prayer did not work only in David's time—it works today as well. My friend John had been diagnosed with a brain tumor, which had grown from the size of a pea to almost the size of a tennis ball. It was huge and pressing in on all kinds of things. He was having blackouts and epileptic fits.

The doctors were baffled by its size. They were afraid to operate at first, so they pumped John full of medication.

When I heard about his situation, I drove a hundred miles to see him. That night, there was a prayer meeting for him in his church. I walked in and slammed into a wall of unbelief. There were more than two hundred people in this prayer meeting, but no unity. Some were binding and casting this thing out, others were cursing it and some were praying, "If it be Your will, do something." There was every shade of prayer one could imagine.

Father, what on earth is going on here? I asked God.

They don't know what I want to do, He answered.

Well, I said, *what do You want me to do?*

I want you to walk around and just find out right now, just in your spirit, just discern those who are waiting and listening, by faith, He said.

I walked around the room and found 35 people who were just being still. I called John and told him that we needed to have a prayer meeting, with these people, in his house the next evening. The end of John's life was drawing close, so there was no time to waste.

The group gathered the next evening, and I explained that we needed to do nothing but worship God in order to change the atmosphere in John's house. "We're going to come to a place where God will tell us what He wants to do for John and his tumor," I said.

We worshiped for more than two hours that night, starting with thanking God, moving into praising Him and eventually stepping into a place of ministering to God. The atmosphere in the room had changed. "Let's meet again tomorrow night," I said.

Again, we met and began worshiping God. After an hour, I stood up and handed everyone a piece of paper and a pen. "Find yourself a quiet place in the house or the gardens and so on, and just sit before the Lord and ask Him what He wants to do for John," I said, giving everyone half an hour. "When you're learning how to hear the Lord, He doesn't speak to you in whole sentences, but in key words and phrases. Just be still before the Lord and let God breathe on you. Whatever comes into your conscious mind, write it down."

When everyone came back, we went around the room and wrote the key words and phrases on a flip chart. As words were repeated, I put a check mark beside them. By the end of it, some of the words had as many as 25 ticks. Taking those oft-repeated words and writing them down again, I asked the intercessors to go back to their quiet place, to meditate on the words and to form them into a prayer.

An hour later, the group came back together, full of excitement and confidence. They marched in like an army, eyes bright, with faces smiling broadly. People were almost jumping on their seats. "Okay," I said. "We'll start reading them out loud, one sentence at a time." I wrote down the first person's opening sentence. "Anyone else get that first sentence?" I asked. Eight or nine people waved their hands. Faith in the room shot up another notch. "Anybody have an approximate to that first sentence?" I asked. Another six people put up their hands. We went through the whole exercise and found that most people had put the words and phrases in the same order. By the end of the evening, the room was hopping. Hearts were so intense that I thought to myself, *I'd better let these guys pray, or they're going to kill me.*

We wrote out a prayer and came to an agreement that this is what we would pray. This is very important—there is one thing to pray and one thing only. What happens with most of us is that we start off praying in our fear and panic and we give God so many choices that the situation overwhelms us. We end up losing heart and quit praying at all.

That night at John's house, we prayed the prayer once, just to keep people from exploding, and set another prayer meeting for the next evening. It was the fourth straight day we had met. That night, I had a tape recorder and transcripts of the prayer ready. "We'll worship the Lord for an hour or so, because He is worth it, and then we're going to pray this same prayer, one by one. But when you come to pray, you have to let your heart and your faith lift totally before God, and you have to pray it with whatever faith, passion, intensity and power you possess." We recorded the prayers onto the tape. You could feel the intensity grow. At the end of the evening, you felt twelve feet tall.

"Okay," I said, after everyone had a turn. "Now we're going to pray until God tells us to stop, because perseverance in prayer is about praying at the same level of passion, power, intensity and faith on the 91st occasion as we did on the first. The same level! We're going to pray, and when you come to the next prayer meeting, you must listen to this tape and come in at that same level."

We actually prayed for John 73 times, but it was like a picnic. We found it incredibly enjoyable. The more we prayed, the more God did—the more confidence John had, and the more relaxed and peaceful his home became. "How can you be like this?" the nurses would ask, and John would tell them about Jesus.

His family, many of whom were unbelievers, asked John how he could live like this. "I know what God is going to do," he answered. I think God did not heal him immediately because He wanted to accomplish all these things first, moving on the hearts of John's family and nurses. John's faith grew to the point where he began to proclaim what God was going to do. He began to minister to the people who were supposed to be ministering to him.

We came to his home the night before the doctors had scheduled him for surgery and prayed in complete confidence. "John, when you go in tomorrow, you need to ask for another CAT scan," I said. "Don't submit to the knife—ask for a CAT scan. There is no operation here."

"We've already done about a dozen," John replied.

"Well, lucky thirteenth," I said. "Ask for a CAT scan. If they don't want to, tell them I'll pay for it."

The next morning, John went in and asked for one more CAT scan. It took some convincing, but finally they did it. There was nothing there. Thinking the scanner was broken, they put John in a cab and took him across town to another hospital. Again John was scanned. Again there was nothing. "There's absolutely nothing," the doctor said. "Not only is there nothing there, but there doesn't seem to be any trace that anything ever was there."

My favorite part of this story was what John told the doctors moments before they gave him the final CAT scan. "You're not going to find anything there," he had said. When he came out, he said, "I told you so." On his medical records, the medical staff added their explanation: "We know that he belongs to a strong, praying community, and we put this down to an act of God."

Our circumstances are not just about the situation being resolved. They are also about us being changed! We are learning to have increased confidence that things will work out for good (see Romans 8:28).

It is not just about my personal good but about people around me seeing something of God in my circumstances. When we know what God wants to do for us, we can then turn our attention to what

God wants to do *in us* and *around us* to others. Now, with crafted prayer taking care of the problem, we are free to pursue the wider purposes of God in our situation.

This is where we can start to become prophetic. Romans 8:28–30 tells us that in every set of circumstances there is a predetermined path for us to follow that is guaranteed to make us more like Christ: "And we know that all things work together for good to those who love God, to those who are the called according to His purpose. For whom He foreknew, He also predestined to be conformed to the image of His Son, that He might be the firstborn among many brethren. Moreover whom He predestined, these He also called; whom He called, these He also justified; and whom He justified, these He also glorified."

We are "predestined to be conformed to the image of His Son" in our set of circumstances. This passage talks about the here and now, not some future heavenly state (when we are all going to be changed in a twinkling of an eye, anyhow!).

A crafted prayer is not a magic formula—it will take a process, over time, to be answered. We are now free to be conformed to the image of Jesus. We are free from the stress of the situation to begin to

interact with God personally to increase our
intimacy and devotional walk.

The questions we must ask as the situation
unfolds are, "What is it that God wants to be for me
now that He could not be at any other time? What is
God doing *in me* to make me more like Jesus? What
else is God doing *through me* to the people around
me as I go through these circumstances?" We must
begin to see the wider purposes of
God at work. These are the "all
things" of Romans 8:28 that we have
typically missed in past situations. If
we pray, in confidence, and the
situation does not change as quickly
as we would like, we must not be disheartened. You
are praying God's will, so learn to persevere, to pray
with joy; the answer *will* come.

> "A prayer may not be answered until all of God's wider objectives have been achieved."
> —Graham Cooke

Often the reason for the wait regarding the answer
is because we are learning to wait on Him. We are
learning how much the Father is for us, according to
Romans 8:31. What are the things the Father wants
to freely give us? There may be more for us to
inherit in this present crisis than we realize. Crisis
now becomes an even greater opportunity to see the
majesty of God.

Why did we have to pray 73 times for John over 5

months? What else was happening as we prayed without ceasing? He changed. He lost his ability to worry and be nervous—things that had characterized his life before. He became more confident and peaceful.

His family radically changed through watching him grow in his new persona and faith. The medical staff were astonished! They began asking searching questions about the Lord, peace and faith.

Work colleagues, friends, neighbors and some church members were shaken by the quality of his faith and his confidence. His unshakable peace shook them all up! People do not read the Bible—they read the people of God. We must not be double-minded (see James 1:5–8) but have a confident conviction of God's nature to us.

crafted prayers develop our character

There are prayers that God has given me in my life and ministry that have saved me. In a ministry like mine, people will often speak against you and criticize you. In an average month, I'll receive several letters disparaging my ministry. These letters can be savage, criticizing everything I am. It is no wonder that more than half of the prophetic people I started out with thirty years ago have had a nervous breakdown, have left the ministry and live in rejection or bitterness.

To deal with these letters, I have a crafted prayer. It is a few sentences that have become the first place I retreat to. "Father, I'm weary of being misunderstood," I pray. "I'm tired of the ungracious scrutiny of others. Hide me, dear Lord, in the secret place of Your presence. Keep me from people who speak about me, but not to me. I'm helpless against the riptide of their words. I cannot defend myself. Refresh my heart to look on them with love. I accept this part of Your cross. Change my heart to speak with Your love, and sculpt my life through these situations. Let their hard words chisel away my roughness, forming Christ."

I pray that and then read the letter. It saves me from getting angry, getting twisted, getting resentful and getting bitter. We should have a joyful, but disciplined, approach to God, because this produces faithfulness in us. I have crafted prayers for my wife, my sons, my daughter, my friends, my church and my enemies. I have a book full of crafted prayers that I am still praying. I use a prayer until the situation changes and then put it into a filing cabinet. It does not matter how difficult a situation is—I can just sit down, open my prayer book and start to pray. There are days when I pray with passion and faith and days where I just pray with whatever I can muster. Usually when I reach the end of the prayer, a smile breaks out on my face.

how to craft your prayers

Jesus was the One who taught us the most about prayer. He said, "Ask, and it will be given to you; seek, and you will find; knock, and it will be opened to you" (Matthew 7:7). He guaranteed our prayers would be answered. Prayer is not rocket science. God just wants us to be confident in prayer.

Paul wrote, "Rejoice in the Lord always. Again I will say, rejoice! Let your gentleness be known to all men. The Lord is at hand. Be anxious for nothing, but in everything by prayer and supplication, with thanksgiving, let your requests be made known to God; and the peace of God, which surpasses all understanding, will guard your hearts and minds through Christ Jesus" (Philippians 4:4–7). We must combine our supplication, our need to know how to pray for a specific situation, with thanksgiving. When we do not know how to pray, we should enter

God's presence with thanksgiving and then ask Him questions:

- ► *So, what are You up to?*
- ► *What's happening here?*
- ► *What is it You want to do?*
- ► *I know You—You're up to something. What is it?*
- ► *What does that look like?*
- ► *What's the plan, Father?*
- ► *What do You want me to do?*

Supplication reminds me of something I used to do with my children, when they were younger. I would often take them out on day trips to give my wife a chance to, well, recover from all of us. We would pile into the car, with all of the necessary provisions, and just go. I wouldn't tell them where, which drove them to ask endless questions: "Where are we going, Dad? What are we doing? What's going to happen?" After a few minutes, I would give them my map, with the destination marked. God reminded me of these day trips when He was teaching me about prayer.

Grae, I have a plan, He would say.

What is it? Where are we going? I would answer back impulsively.

I want you to know.

So I would worship and ask God to show me His ways and teach me His path. His answers have become the foundation for all my crafted prayers. Today, my supplication looks like this: *Father, I praise You for this situation. I know You have a plan and a purpose for me. I give You thanks that You are with me and that You are for me. I ask You to show me Your ways, teach me Your paths, show me Your will, O Lord, that I may become conformed to the image of Jesus in this situation. Show me Your will that I may confidently and joyfully cooperate with You.*

And then I am simply still. And I listen. And I meditate on God, waiting for Him to speak. He will give you key words and phrases and a sense of His objective. Then He might supplement that with Scripture or pictures. Write everything down as it comes to you. As you do, a peace will fall on you, and a confidence will begin to rise in your spirit.

Prayer should be a joyful experience. Paul wrote, "I thank my God upon every remembrance of you, always in every prayer of mine making request for you all with joy" (Philippians 1:3–4). When we know how God is going to answer our prayer, happiness fills our hearts. When people know what God is going to do, they cannot wipe the smiles off their faces. As a Church, we know how to pray with depression all too well, but prayer with joy is the experience we are destined to have. For too long, we have prayed with anxiety, with fear, with nervousness, with unbelief, with doubt. It is time for joy to return to our prayer life.

Prayer is a paradox—two apparently conflicting ideas contained in the same truth. Yes, God wants us to be spontaneous and move freely in His will, but He also wants us to plan, to be purposeful, intentional and rehearsed. The Bible is a great example of that dedication to order, a Book that took centuries of divine planning and purpose.

> "Call to Me and I will show you great and mighty things which you do not know."
> —God, through Jeremiah

Spontaneity has become an unnecessary crutch for the Spirit-filled Church. We have relied solely on being spontaneous, as if God abhors planning. Yet it is when we plan, are purposeful, rehearsed and have written our revelation down that we are released to be truly spontaneous. If all we have is off-the-cuff spirituality, we will never mature in our faith. In fact, this spontaneity makes us inflexible to the Spirit. How do we pray when our heart gives out? How do we remember what we prayed yesterday? True spontaneous spirituality arises out of a heart soaked and prepared by a relationship with the Holy

Spirit. Knowing that God is intentional, I can be sure that I am not quenching the Holy Spirit when I use crafted prayers. God is prepared and has planned well—we must return the compliment.

Simplifying our faith is also helpful in prayer. I try to be childlike in my confession of faith: "God said; I believe it; that jolly well settles it." Jesus did the same: "'You shall love the LORD your God with all your heart, with all your soul, and with all your mind.' This is the first and great commandment. And the second is like it: 'You shall love your neighbor as yourself.' On these two commandments hang all the Law and the Prophets" (Matthew 22:37–40). Jesus was telling His disciples that when their faith was tested and their hearts began to fail, there were just two simple commands to follow: "Love Me, and love the person next to you."

Crafted prayer works especially well in families and small groups, as intercessors are able to encourage one another, compare notes and seek answers together. As Jesus said, "Again I say to you that if two of you agree on earth concerning anything that they ask, it will be done for them by My Father in heaven. For where two or three are gathered together in My name, I am there in the midst of them" (Matthew 18:19–20). Together, we

Learning to Stand

My child, in this next season I am going to radically change
   your perspective.
You will begin to understand both the Power that is behind you
   as well as the Power that is within you.

I will teach you how to stand on the word of your God.
Know that as you stand on My word, so at the same moment
   you stand on the evil one.
I have put a sword in your hand and confession and
   proclamation upon your lips.

You are learning to stand in the Presence of God and those I
   send to assist you.
Know that you are being watched over and protected.
Therefore I say to you ... stand up, stand upon, and stand
   against and you shall prevail.

can discover and pray into what God wants to do through every situation.

What is an effective prayer? Very simply, it is a prayer God gives us permission to pray, prayed fervently, full of passion and power. These are the PUSH (Pray Until Something Happens) prayers mentioned earlier. Crafted prayer is about intention, aligning our request to God's will. There are prayers we need to write about our circumstances. There are prayers we need to write about our family and friends.

Throughout the rest of this book, you will find numerous exercises and examples to help you write your own crafted prayers. I strongly encourage you to work through this book, both individually and in a group, and create a journal of your own prayers. These prayers will be sustenance for your prayer life and provide marvelous answers and strength in your time of need.

conclusion

Prayer, done correctly, will stir up a spirit of boldness in our lives. Before we know it, we will have slipped into proclaiming the greatness and wisdom of God. There is nothing like the rush of faith and adrenaline that happens when people are praying and suddenly shift gears into proclamation. It is as if they have hit the mother lode and have begun to proclaim God's will prophetically for the situation they are praying for. This spirit of proclamation is part of our DNA as a Christian. When we know God's will, we enter into a certainty of the outcome. The confidence of the Holy Spirit fills us, and we become God's voice in a specific situation.

> "I want to know God's thoughts. The rest are details."
> —Albert Einstein

Wonderfully, we are not praying to get an answer—we are praying with the answer. Because we know what God wants to do, we are free to follow the process God has ordained for us in the circumstances He has allowed.

It is time to use prayer as a weapon. We must grow up in our intercession, becoming the joyful, confident men and women God has destined us to be. Our prayer lives can be the most richly rewarding part of our walk with God if we just take the time to enter His presence with thanksgiving and still ourselves until we can rest in His secret place. Then we can ask the Holy Spirit to reveal to us what the conversation in heaven is over our situation, and we can craft a prayer that will be answered.

appendix 1

General Preparation (Ecclesiastes 5:1–7)
1. Keep "updating" your information about God's love, His purposes, His ways. Be reading and meditating on relevant Bible passages (2 Timothy 3:14–17).
2. Review and meditate on crafted prayers in the Bible (Matthew 6:9–15; John 17; Romans 12:14–21; Ephesians 1:15–23; 3:14–19; 1 Timothy 2:1–2).

Steps for an Individual
1. Be thankful to God for His promises toward you (Jeremiah 29:11–14).
2. Be thankful to God for what He has already done (Philippians 4:4–7).

3. Begin to worship God as your thanksgiving brings you into His presence (Psalm 100).

4. Come to a place of stillness inside—prepare your heart to listen to God (Psalm 46).

5. Clarify and simplify the current area for crafted prayer.

6. Ask the Lord to show you what He wants to accomplish, first, in the situation, and second, in you through this time.

7. Seek to discover what the Father, Son and Holy Spirit are praying for this situation (Hebrews 7:23–25; Romans 8:22–30).

8. Gather the thoughts and words God gives you. Write them down.

9. Take these thoughts and words back to the Lord, and pray for further clarification. Write down any further insight you receive.

10. In the place of stillness, craft a prayer that includes the key elements (words, ideas and phrases) God has made known to you. Do not rush or push.

11. Take your crafted prayer back to the Lord. Ask for confirmation or alteration, if necessary, until you are as confident as you can be that you have the mind of God on how to pray.

12. Move into a time of proclamation of what God will do based on your faith in whom God is and your understanding of His will.

13. Accept the fact that God will do things in His own time and His own way!

14. As God leads you, continue to pray and proclaim with confidence what God has shown you until resolution comes.

Steps for a Group

1. Be thankful to God for His promises towards you (Jeremiah 29:11–14).

2. Be thankful to God for what He has already done (Philippians 4:4–7).

3. Begin to worship God as your thanksgiving brings you into His presence (Psalm 100).

4. Come to a place of stillness inside—prepare your heart to listen to God (Psalm 46).

5. Clarify and simplify the area for crafted prayer.

6. Ask the Lord to show you what He wants to accomplish in the situation and in the life of the group or church through this time. Also ask Him what He wants to accomplish in your life.

7. Seek to discover what the Father, Son and Holy Spirit are praying for this situation (Hebrews 7:23–25; Romans 8:22–30).

8. Individually gather the thoughts and words God gives you. Write them down.

9. Come together and share the words and phrases you believe God has revealed to you. Identify any that have been received by a number of group members.

10. Take these common thoughts and words back to the Lord and pray for further clarification. Write down any further insight you receive.

11. Together, enter that place of stillness and craft a prayer that includes the key elements (words, ideas and phrases) God has made known to you. Do not rush or push.

12. Take your crafted prayer back to the Lord. Ask for confirmation or alteration, if necessary, until you are as confident as you can be that you have the mind of God on how to pray.

13. Move into a time of proclamation of what God will do based on your faith in whom God is and your understanding of His will.

14. Accept the fact that God will do things in His own time and His own way!

15. Individually, as God leads you, continue to pray and proclaim with confidence what God has shown you until resolution comes.

appendix 2

1. Begin with thanksgiving and worship.
2. Come to stillness inside—prepare your heart to listen to God.
3. Clarify and simplify the area for crafted prayer:

   . . . .

   . . . .

   . . . .

4. Ask the Lord to show you what He wants to accomplish in the situation, group and yourself.

   . . . .

   . . . .

   . . . .

5. Ask to be shown what is the desire and prayer of the Father, Son and Holy Spirit.

6. Gather the thoughts and words God gives you—
   write them down.

   . . . .
   . . . .
   . . . .

7. Come together and share the words and phrases
   you believe God has revealed to you. Which are
   common to a number of you?

   . . . .
   . . . .
   . . . .

8. Take these common thoughts and words to the
   Lord and pray for further clarification. Write
   down any further insights you receive.

   . . . .
   . . . .
   . . . .

9. Together, enter that place of stillness and craft
   a prayer.

   . . . .
   . . . .
   . . . .

10. Take your completed group-crafted prayer back
    to the Lord for clarification.

11. Move into a time of proclamation of what God
    will do.

12. Accept the fact that God will do things in His own time and way.
13. Individually, as God leads you, continue to pray and proclaim with confidence what God has shown you until resolution comes.

appendix 3

1. Begin with thanksgiving and worship.
2. Come to stillness inside–prepare your heart to listen to God.
3. Clarify and simplify the area for crafted prayer:

   . . . .

   . . . .

   . . . .

4. Ask the Lord to show you what He wants to accomplish in the situation.

   . . . .

   . . . .

   . . . .

5. Ask to be shown what is the desire and prayer of the Father, Son and Holy Spirit.

6. Gather the thoughts and words God gives you—write them down.

. . . .
. . . .
. . . .

7. Bring your list of thoughts and words to the Lord and pray for further clarification. Write down any further insights you receive.

. . . .
. . . .
. . . .

8. Enter that place of stillness and craft a prayer that contains the key words and phrases you have received.

. . . .
. . . .
. . . .

9. Take your completed crafted prayer back to the Lord for clarification.

10. Move into a time of proclamation of what God will do.

11. Accept the fact that God will do things in His own time and way.

12. As God leads you, continue to pray and proclaim with confidence what God has shown you until resolution comes.

appendix 4

stillness exercise

Being still is a vital part of hearing the conversation going on in heaven over your life and situation. Ironically, the time you most need stillness is when everything is chaotic around you. Peace is like having an equalizing pressure inside you that keeps you from being crumpled by outside pressure.

Try this exercise in being still:

1. Find a comfortable place.
2. Put on a worship CD for a few minutes. Sing along.
3. Slow your breathing down. Inhale and exhale deeply.
4. Just be silent before the Lord.

5. If your thoughts wander, bring them back to God.

6. If you have a stray thought, turn it into something positive. For example, you might suddenly think, *I need milk for the kids tomorrow.* Turn that thought into a prayer of thanksgiving for your children and God's provision.

By chasing your stray thoughts down, you train your mind to be still before the Lord. There will come a point when your thoughts will be under control. Paul wrote, "For the weapons of our warfare are not carnal but mighty in God for pulling down strongholds, casting down arguments and every high thing that exalts itself against the knowledge of God, *bringing every thought into captivity to the obedience of Christ,* and being ready to punish all disobedience when your obedience is fulfilled" (2 Corinthians 10:4–6, my italics).

appendix 5

When crafting a prayer for yourself, it is important to ask God for an inheritance word. These are usually passages of Scripture that He highlights and asks you to meditate on for long periods of time. As a son or daughter of the Almighty, you have an inheritance, and God wants you to know what it is. Jesus Himself, after spending forty days and forty nights being tested in the wilderness (see Luke 4), returned to civilization and went straight to a synagogue. He opened the Scriptures to Isaiah 61 and proclaimed this passage as His inheritance. "Today this Scripture is fulfilled in your hearing," He said (verse 21).

God will give you an inheritance word, if He

hasn't done so already. The word will set you up to
discover what you are going to experience during
the next stage of your journey of faith. It may be
two or three passages of the Bible, but He will put it
in your heart, and it is your inheritance. Ask for it.
When you receive a passage, do not read anything
else for a while. Read it and reread it. Memorize it, if
you can. Take it apart, piece by piece. Study it. Look
it up in Bible commentaries. Research the original
language. Ask God to illuminate His truth in it.
Every ounce of revelation is yours to experience. This
passage is part of the conversation in heaven about
you, so use it for all it's worth. Then write a crafted
prayer about it, asking for the things that have been
laid out as promises in your inheritance word.

Many years ago, God gave me an inheritance
word for the next phase of my life, through Psalm
91. *I want you to study this, and I don't want you to
read anything else in Scripture for the next nine
months,* God told me one day. *Grae, I want you to
read it, study it, memorize it. Everything in that
psalm is yours to experience.* I remember that after
three months of reading the same sixteen verses, I
was desperate for a little bit of Timothy. I flipped to
the New Testament, and immediately my eyes went
out of focus. *What did I say to you?* the Lord chided.

I found the bookmark and returned to Psalm 91, and my eyes went back to normal. *Grae, I need you to get this,* the Lord said. *This is your Bible right now. This psalm is everything I want to show you. You must come into this so I can do what I want to do.*

Psalm 91 is powerful:

> He who dwells in the secret place of the Most High
> Shall abide under the shadow of the Almighty.
> I will say of the LORD, "He is my refuge and my
>   fortress;
> My God, in Him I will trust."

> Surely He shall deliver you from the snare of the
>   fowler
> And from the perilous pestilence.
> He shall cover you with His feathers,
> And under His wings you shall take refuge;
> His truth shall be your shield and buckler.
> You shall not be afraid of the terror by night,
> Nor of the arrow that flies by day,
> Nor of the pestilence that walks in darkness,
> Nor of the destruction that lays waste at noonday.

> A thousand may fall at your side,
> And ten thousand at your right hand;
> But it shall not come near you.
> Only with your eyes shall you look,
> And see the reward of the wicked.

Because you have made the LORD, who is my refuge,
Even the Most High, your dwelling place,
No evil shall befall you,
Nor shall any plague come near your dwelling;
For He shall give His angels charge over you,
To keep you in all your ways.
In their hands they shall bear you up,
Lest you dash your foot against a stone.
You shall tread upon the lion and the cobra,
The young lion and the serpent you shall trample
    underfoot.

"Because he has set his love upon Me, therefore I
    will deliver him;
I will set him on high, because he has known My
    name.
He shall call upon Me, and I will answer him;
I will be with him in trouble;
I will deliver him and honor him.
With long life I will satisfy him,
And show him My salvation."

I have written several crafted prayers out of this passage and seen God, time after time, turn back the attacks of the enemy. God has allowed Satanists and the occult to come against me, to lure them into a trap He has set—for them! Psalm 91 was a test for me, to learn how to live in God's refuge, sovereignty and majesty. A Satanist once took a seat next to me on an airplane, with a specific assignment to curse me. When we reached our cruising altitude of 35,000 feet, he introduced himself.

"I'm a Satanist," he said. "My whole coven has been given a commission to curse you to death."

I looked at him—he was dressed like a successful businessman. I smiled.

"Okay," I said. "Let's hear it." He proceeded to curse me, my health and my ministry. It was interesting how his face and language changed. His eyes became hooded and his voice low and sibilant. Finally, he ceased. I had held his eyes the whole time.

"Is that it?" I said, feigning disappointment. "The last Satanist to curse me was much better. The Lord really used his words to bless me. I was hoping this would be another such situation. Every word you say against me, the Lord will turn into a blessing. So why not think about it for a while, take a deep breath, and start again."

He declined. I continued the conversation. "Actually, you're not really here to curse me," I said. "You're here because the Holy Spirit has an assignment on your life. You're here to listen to the message that the Lord is pursuing you with love. He will be to you like the hound of heaven—you cannot get away. How do you like those apples?"

The Satanist got up, spoke with the flight attendant and switched seats. Bless his heart. I had confidence in what God was going to do, because I knew my inheritance. I knew God had promised me that no evil would befall me and that I would trample the lion, the cobra, the young lion and the serpent. That is the power of an inheritance word made into a crafted prayer.

Let's pray together that God will give you an inheritance word.

"Father, I thank You. Of all people in the earth, we are the most confident. We're the happiest people on earth because of who You are. We represent Your Kingdom of joy. I thank You that You're only acquainted with grief, that You are the happiest person that lives.

"Father, I pray in the name of Jesus that You will give us a spirit of wisdom and revelation in the knowledge of You. I ask that You will show us our inheritance for the next stage of our journey, and I pray that You will enable us to study, to think into that, to meditate on Your word. I pray, Holy Spirit, that You would give us inspiration and insight into that word. Bring us into an experience of that word through the circumstances You allow, so that we are established in the inheritance You show us. Help us to grow rapidly, to be expanded and to go deep in who You are.

"Raise us to a higher level in the Spirit. So, I pray, reveal our inheritance in word form and inspire us to seize it, so that our hearts will be filled with Your confidence and certainty. In Jesus' name, Amen."

appendix 6

There are many prayer triggers in the Bible, crafted prayers God has handed down through the ages. These are prayers earthed in Scripture, which get an automatic yes and amen:

► "Be merciful to me, a sinner" (Luke 18:13).
► "Set my mind on what the Holy Spirit wants today" (Romans 8:5).
► "Let me be led by the Holy Spirit today" (Romans 8:14).
► "Control my life by Your Spirit" (Romans 8:10).
► "Help me put to death the deeds of flesh that Your life may reign in me" (Romans 8:13).
► "Help me, Father, to count myself dead to sin but alive to You" (Romans 6:11).

- "Show me Your ways, Lord. Teach me Your paths. Lead me in the way everlasting" (Psalm 25:4–5).
- "Let me hunger and thirst for Your righteousness" (Matthew 5:6).
- "Renew my mind, O God. Let me love You with all my heart, soul, mind and strength" (Mark 12:30).
- "One thing I ask, Lord—to live in Your house and behold Your beauty" (Psalm 27:4).

Exercise

I want to challenge you to sit down, over the next few months, with a group of friends and seek God for crafted prayers for your life. Go through every area of your life and ask Him, "What is it I'm supposed to be praying in this situation?" Find out what the Lord is doing in each area. If there is a stronghold of sin in your life, pray, "This thing has always beaten me, so how do I beat it? What is the prayer I can use to release the power and presence of God in my life?"

Write a prayer about your own relationship with God, asking Him for what you want in your life.

about the author

Graham Cooke is married to Heather, and they have three adult children, Ben, Seth and Sophie. Graham and Heather divide their time between Southampton, England, and Vacaville, California.

Graham is a member of the apostolic team of c.net (Cornerstone), a network of ministries and a family of churches spanning 44 nations. He is a member of Community Church in Southampton (UK), responsible for the prophetic and training program, and works with team leader Billy Kennedy. In California, he is part of the pastoral leadership team and works with senior pastor David Crone. He has responsibility for Insight, a training program within the church and for the region.

Graham, a popular conference speaker, is well-known for his training programs on the prophetic, spiritual warfare, intimacy with God, leadership and spirituality. He functions as a consultant within c.net (and beyond), specifically helping churches make the transition from one dimension of calling to a higher level of vision and ministry. He has a passion to build prototype churches that can fully reach our postmodern society.

A strong part of Graham's ministry is in producing finances and resources to help the poor, and he supports many projects around the world. He also financially supports and helps to underwrite church planting, leadership development, evangelism and health and rescue projects in the developing world. If you wish to become a financial partner for the sake of missions, please contact Graham's office, where his personal assistant, Carole Shiers, will be able to assist you.

Graham has many prayer partners who play a significant part in his ministry. For more information, check his website (below).

Graham has written four other books, *Developing Your Prophetic Gifting* (Chosen), *A Divine Confrontation ... Birth Pangs of the New Church* (Destiny Image), *Crafted Prayer* (Chosen) and *The Secret of a Powerful Inner Life* (Chosen).

You can learn more about Graham Cooke at:

Graham Cooke
P.O. Box 91
Southampton
SO15 5ZE
United Kingdom

Website: www.grahamcooke.com